UNIT 17

A US Marine's Comic Impressions of Life on a VA Psych Ward

Harry Hughes

UNIT 17: A US Marine's Comic Impressions
of Life on a VA Psych Ward

© Copyright 2017 Harry Hughes

All rights reserved

ISBN: 978-1-941066-16-4

Book and cover design by
Jo-Anne Rosen

Wordrunner Press
Petaluma, California

This compilation is dedicated to
Ruhama Veltfort,
without whose encouragement
this little book might never have
seen the light of print.

Unit 17

As an aimless seventeen-year-old, 1965 Long Island high school graduate, I understood few options available for advancing myself in our complex world. Most guys my age advanced to college, sought blue-collar jobs and married young, or enlisted in the Armed Forces. I had not yet felt suited for university life and possessed no interest in settling down into a placid vocation. So, it is not surprising that two days following my graduation ceremony, I arrived by bus with a cargo of fellow lost souls at Marine Corps Recruit Depot, Parris Island, South Carolina.

At age nineteen, and without a clue of what combat had in store for me, I found myself ducking shrapnel, dodging incoming fire, witnessing carnage, and yes, eating lousy food and engaging in meaningless work details. Upon release from the Marines, something within me had changed. Fortunately, I was able to proceed with a satisfying life of travel, marriage, advanced education, authorship, and realized music accomplishments. Yet, the Vietnam experience had fractured a critical I-beam supporting my mental wellbeing and in 1997, I admitted myself to a Veterans Administration Medical Center for treatment of clinical depression.

During my three-week stay there, I received writing material from a visiting friend. She suggested that I compile a journal describing life on a psychiatric ward. But, I found words inadequate to convey that experience. So, I rotated the writing pad sideways and began to draw pictures, cartoons actually, that represented my impressions of life among fellow veterans in a very unique environment. The effort resulted in a collection of one hundred cartoons titled Unit 17. This work is not an attempt to ridicule or in any way disparage the dedicated men and women who serve in the Armed Forces or those who treat our veterans for mental and emotional disorders upon arrival home. All names and renderings of patients and staff appearing in these drawings are fictitious, as is the name of the unit. This work is copyrighted, all rights reserved.

© Hughes 1997

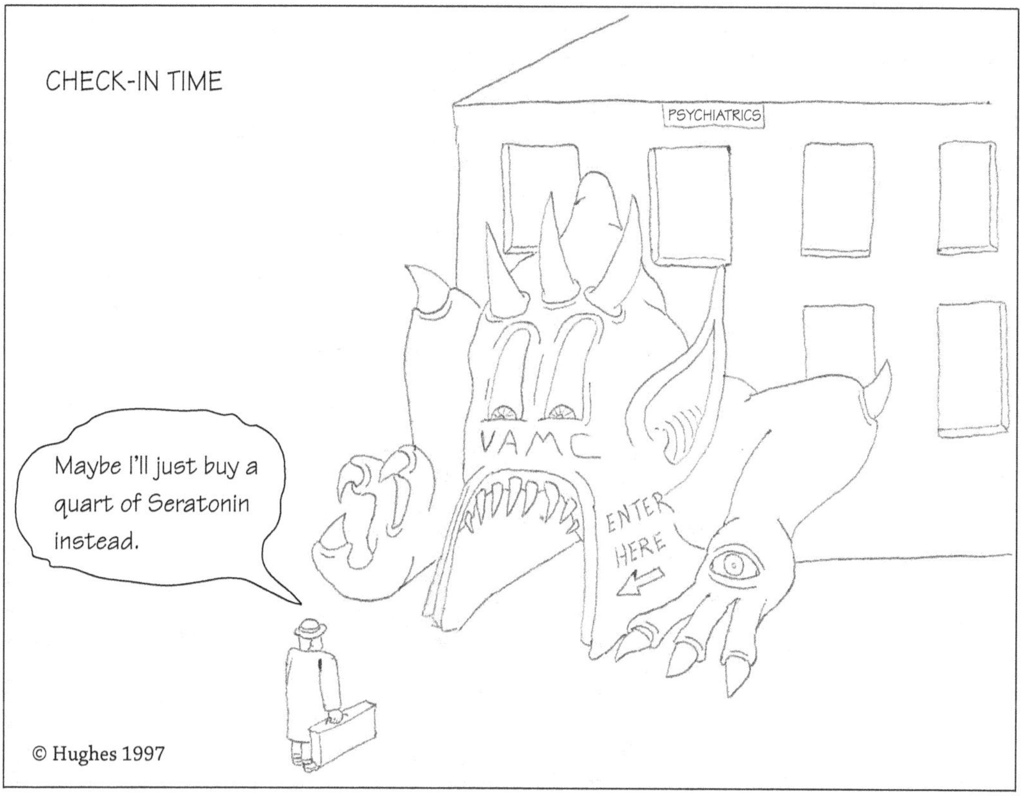

MR. MECKLINDALE FINALLY COMPLETES
THE MILTON-BRADLEY SPECIAL TWO-PIECE JIG-SAW PUZZLE... ALMOST.

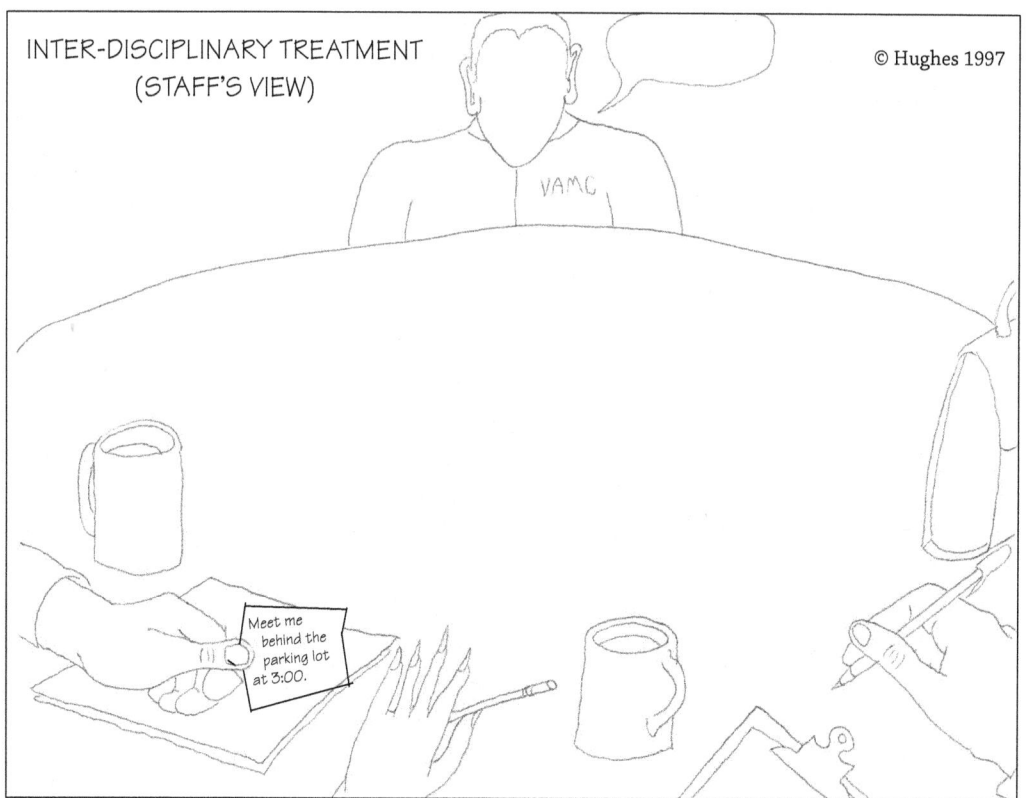

WAITING FOR THE AMERICAN LEGION-SPONSORED PIZZA PARTY

PIZZA PARTY

© Hughes 1997

LIFE ON UNIT 17 CAN SOMETIMES TURN OUT SWELL. CHARLES HOBBES LIKE GIVING WEDGIES, AND THE PLUTCHIK BROTHERS LIKE GETTING THEM.

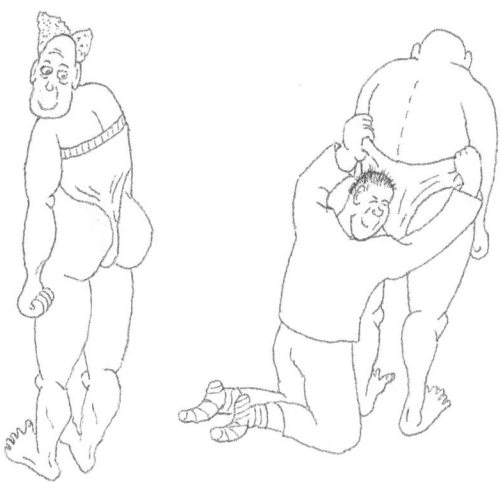

© Hughes 1997

BURL DIGGS PRACTICES FOR HIS FIRST AA MEETING.

My name is Burl and
I'm an albino
My name is Burl and
I'm an altruist
My name is Burl and
I'm an alligator
My name is Burl and
I'm an almond
My name is Burl and
I'm an alka-seltzer
My name is Burl and
I'm an alien
My name is Burl and
I'm an algorithm
My name is Burl and
I'm an alibi
My name is Burl and
I'm an Algonquin
My name is Burl and
I'm an alchemist

© Hughes 1997

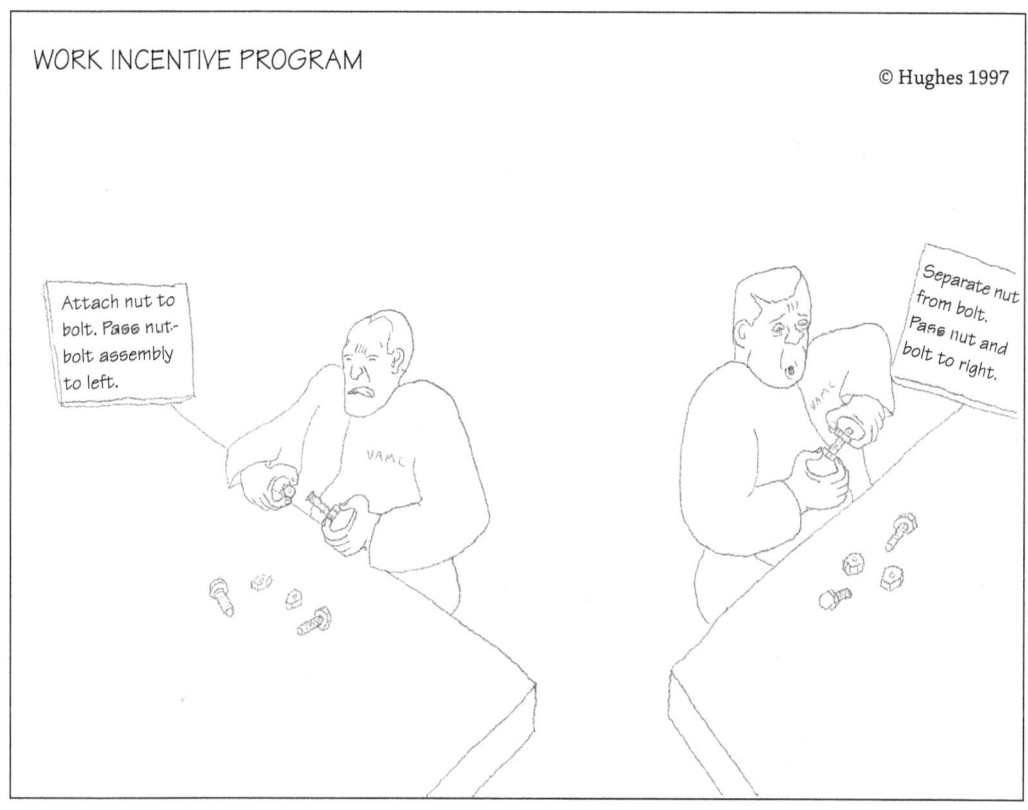

IN A PRIVATE MOMENT, FLOYD HOWE FIGURES OUT THE UNIVERSE.

EVERY THURSDAY MORNING, PASTOR MULLINS, A MINISTER OF GOD'S WORD, COMES OVER FROM THE UNITED METHODIST CHURCH AND READS FROM SCRIPTURE.

EVERY FRIDAY EVENING, LOU DUFFY'S SISTER LOLLY, A PROFESSIONAL DANCER, COMES OVER FROM CLUB KITTY AND LICKS HER OWN BREASTS.

© Hughes 1997

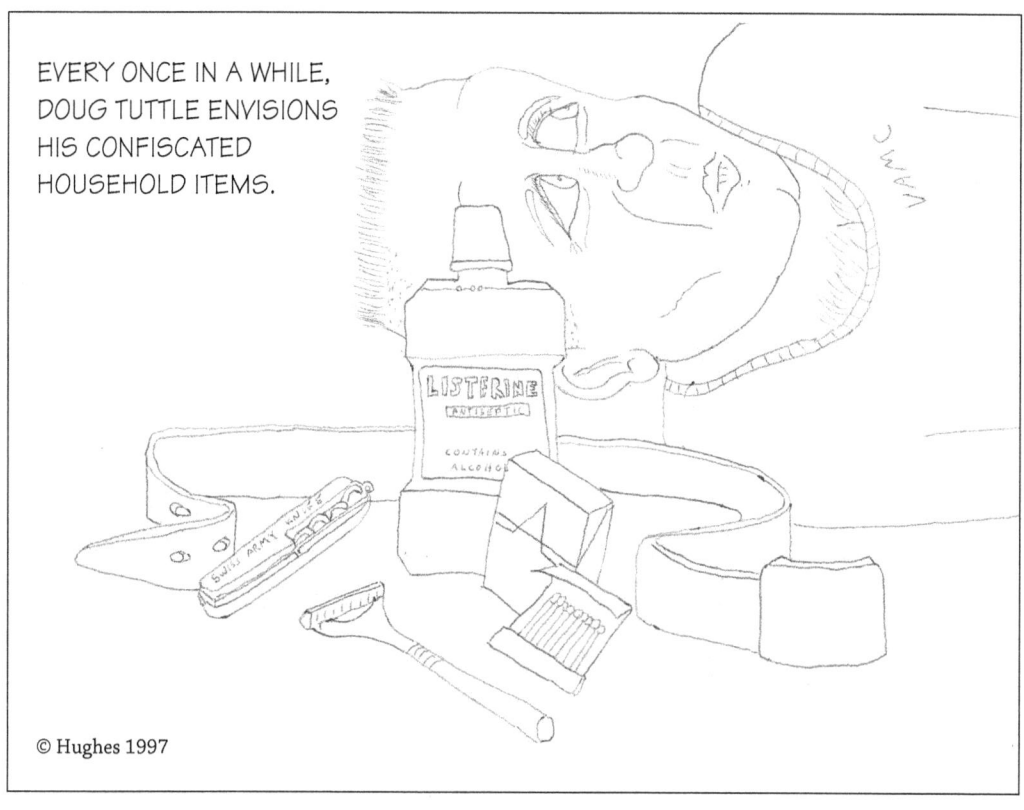

EVERY ONCE IN A WHILE, DOUG TUTTLE ENVISIONS HIS CONFISCATED HOUSEHOLD ITEMS.

© Hughes 1997

NIGHT NURSE CANDY PILQUIST FINDS TIME TO ERECT A FANCIFUL THEME PARK FROM DOUG TUTTLE'S BELONGINGS.

© Hughes 1997

TIRED OF HIS GREEN PAJAMAS, LIONEL GIACOMETTI ASSEMBLES AN OUTFIT TO HIS OWN LIKING.

THE REASON NURSE DONAHUE WAS FIRED

WHEN THOSE SUFFERING FROM ECHOLALIA ARE PAIRED, INFINITE REGRESSION INEVITABLY FOLLOWS.

CONFIDENCE BUILDING

UNIT 17 | 17

UNIT 17 | 19

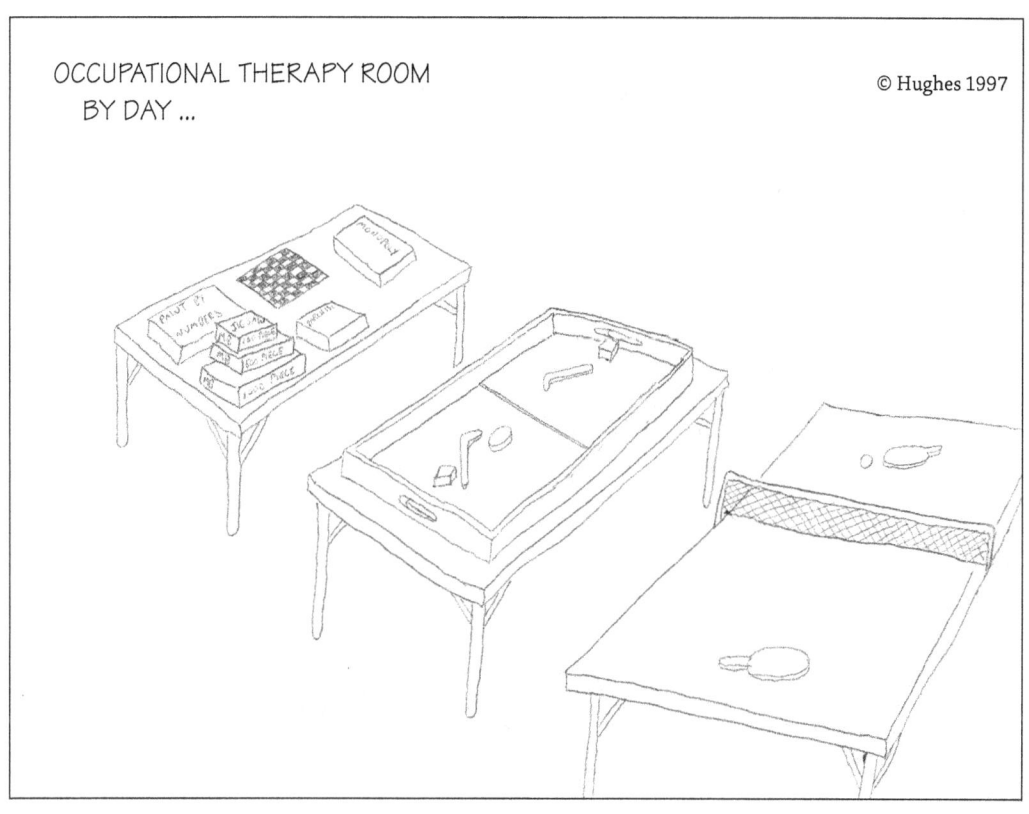

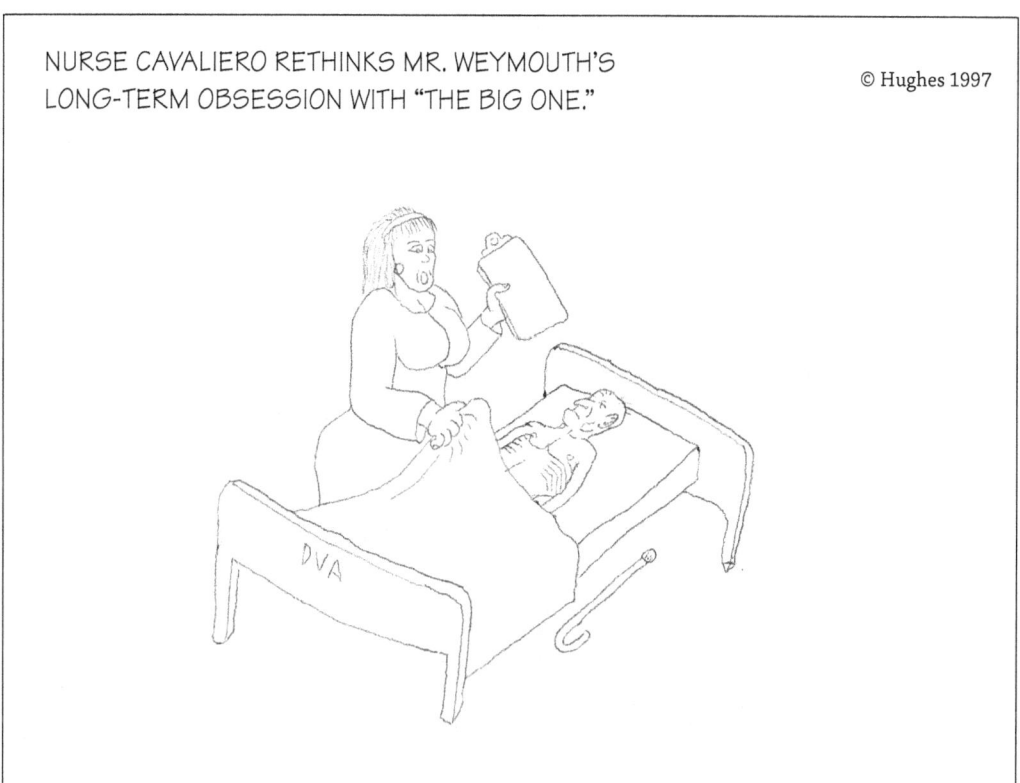

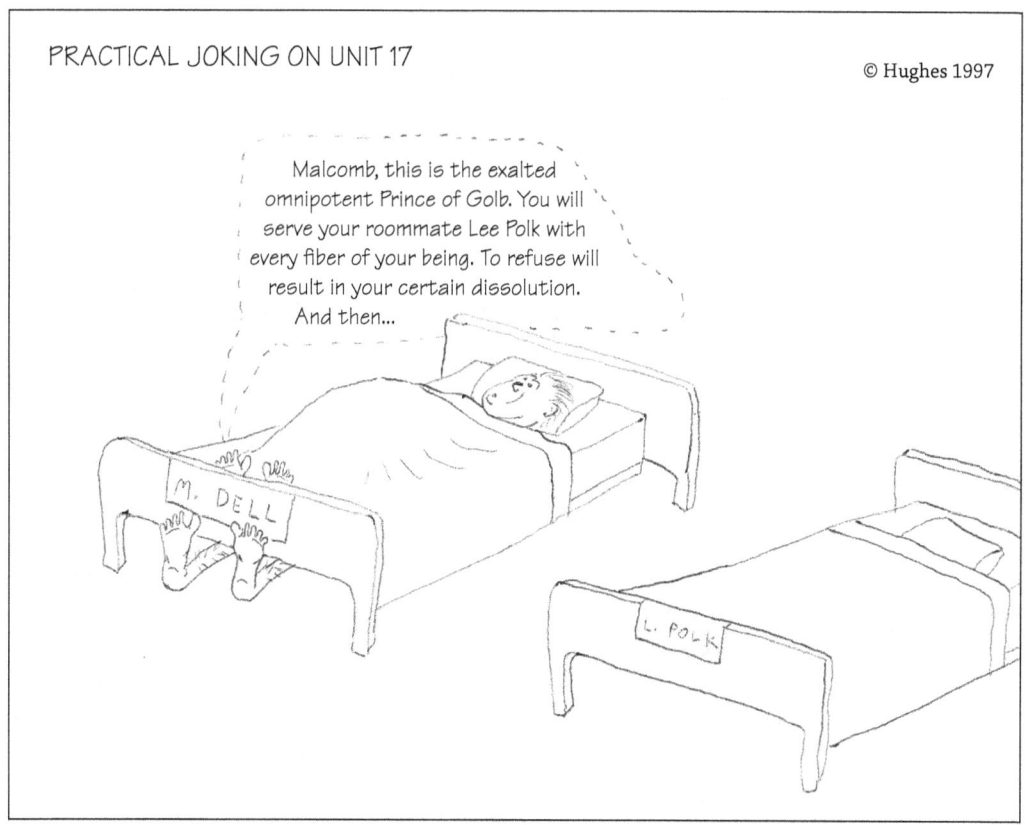

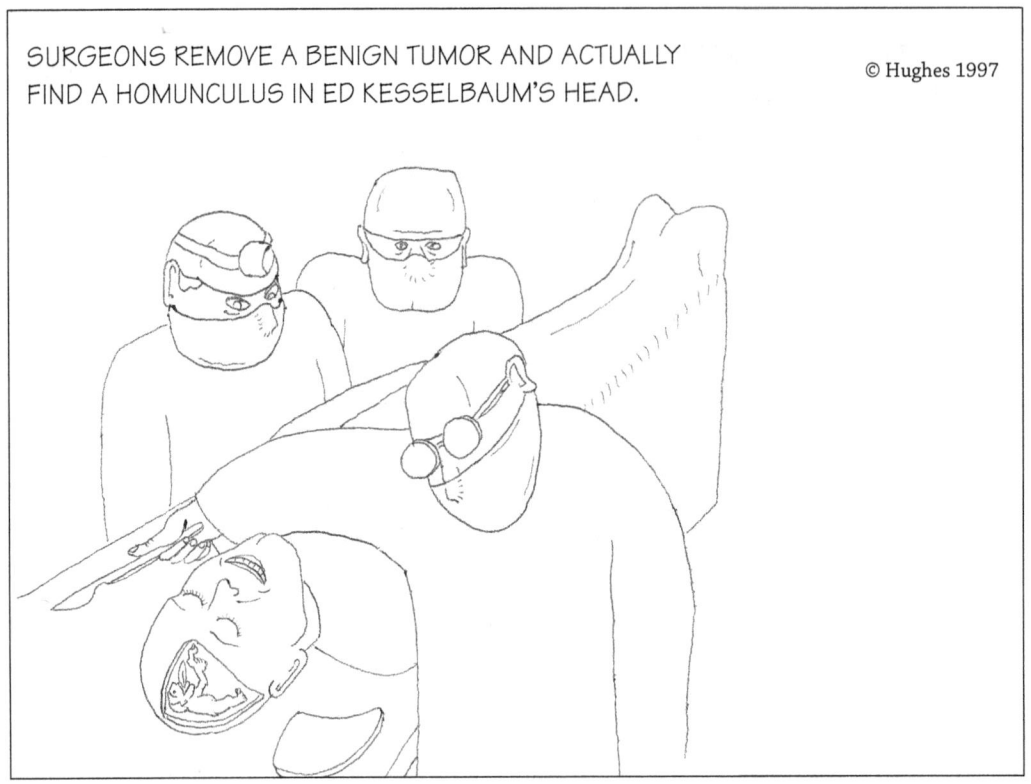

SURGEONS REMOVE A BENIGN TUMOR AND ACTUALLY FIND A HOMUNCULUS IN ED KESSELBAUM'S HEAD.

© Hughes 1997

PATTY HEWLETT, THE ONLY FEMALE PATIENT ON UNIT 17, IS AFFORDED HER OWN ROOM .... SORT OF.

© Hughes 1997

HUMOR ON UNIT 17

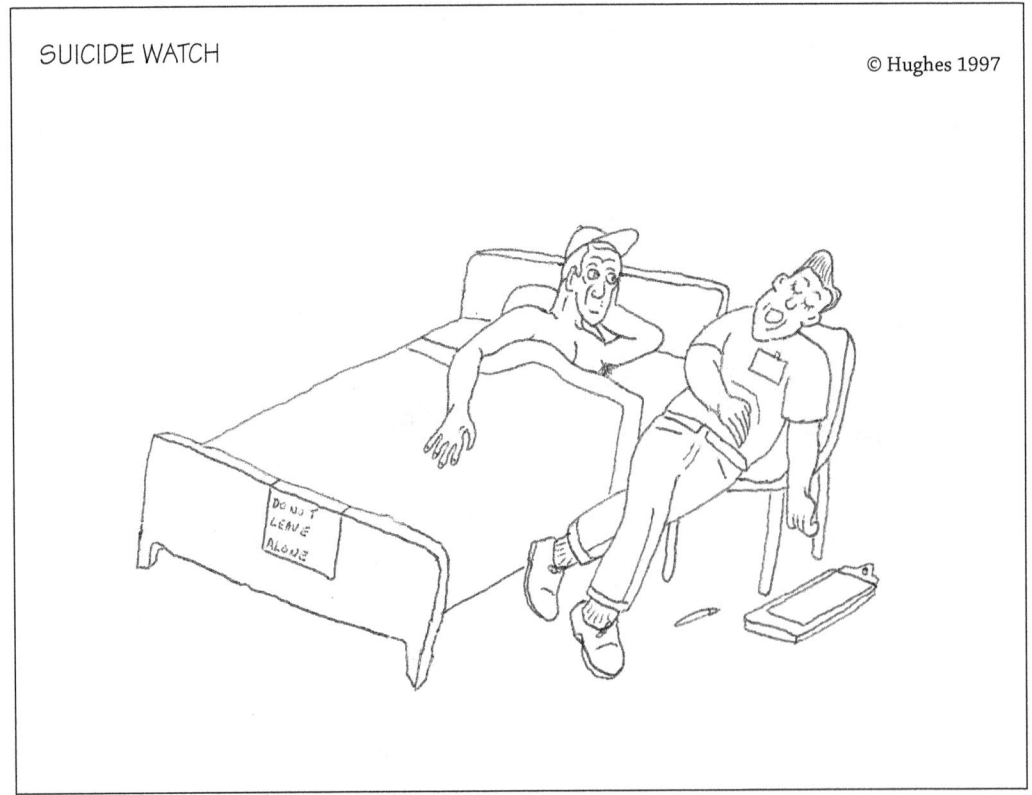

BELIEVING HIMSELF TO BE A G.I. JOE ACTION FIGURE, MURRAY HIRSCHFIELD PLOTS TO ESCAPE UNIT 17 BY HIDING UNDER A PLATE COVER.

© Hughes 1997

SOME ENIGMAS CANNOT BE UNRAVELED, LIKE WHY BALDWIN GRAND WILL ONLY SLEEP UNDER THE REC ROOM PIANO.

© Hughes 1997

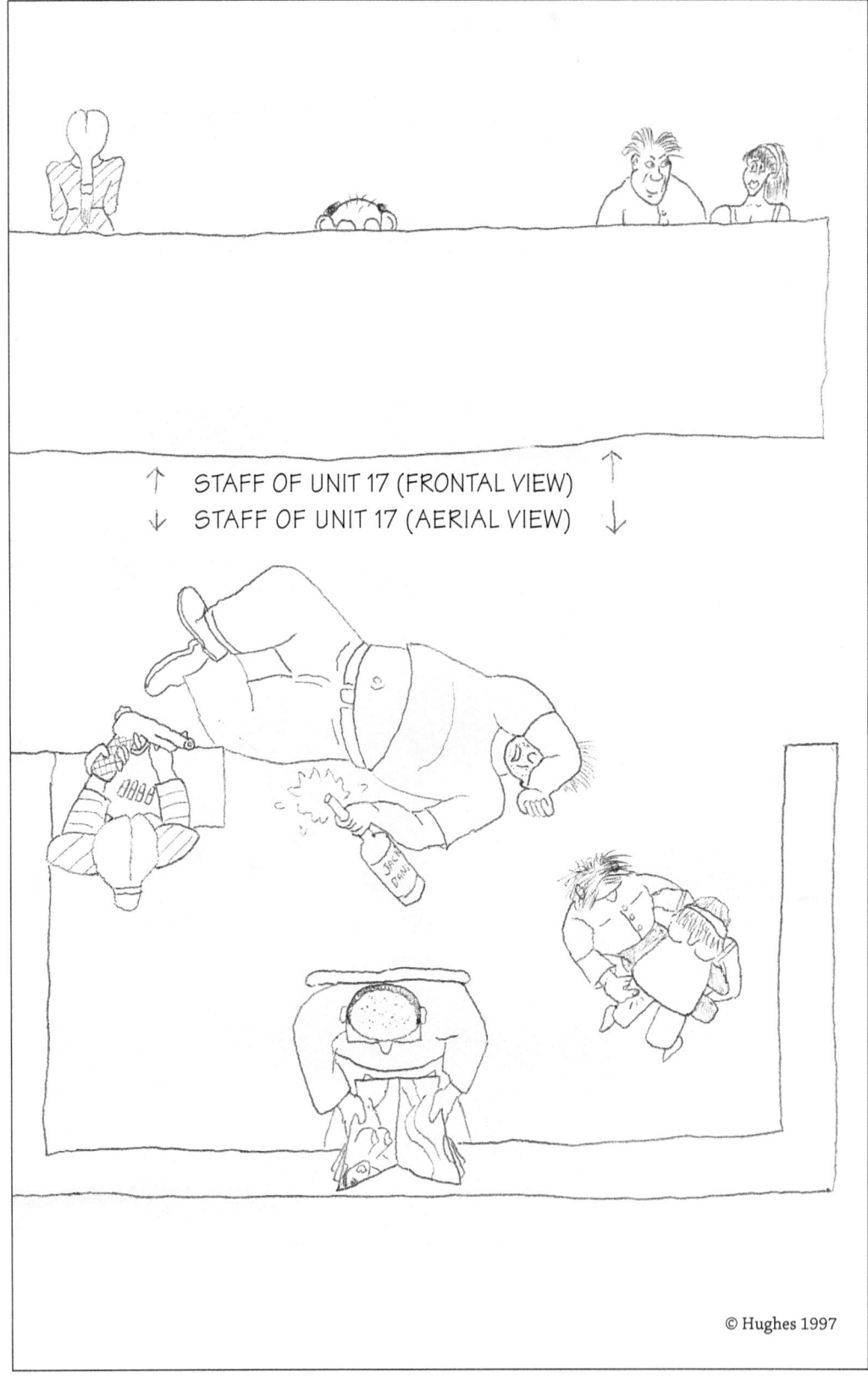

EDGAR EBEL'S RECURRING ERASER HEAD NIGHTMARE

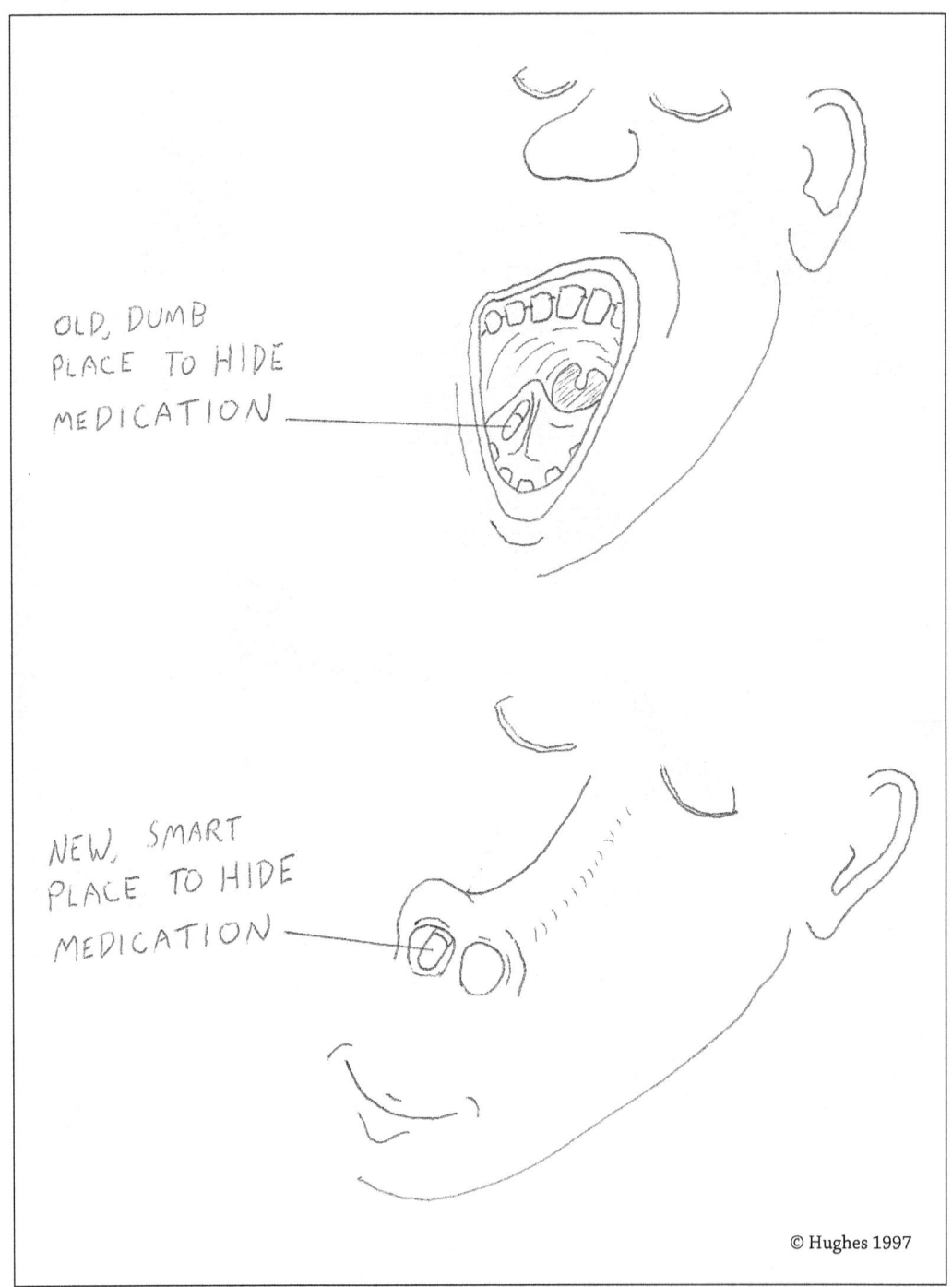

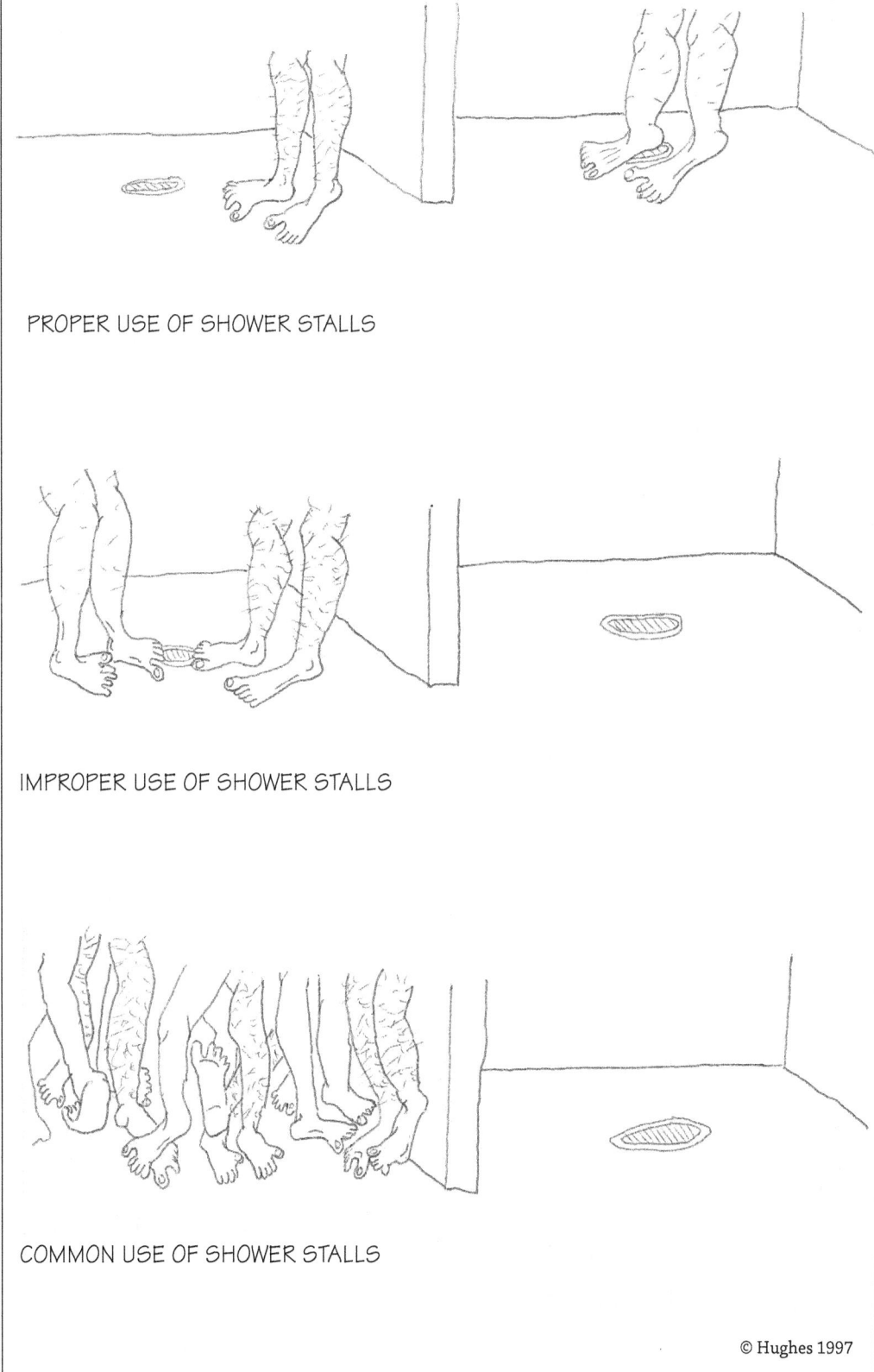

SELF-CONFESSED BIGOT, MIKE BOYLE, LEARNS RACIAL TOLERANCE THROUGH AN APPROPRIATE VEHICLE.

© Hughes 1997

Index of Captions

30 years after the fact, Kevin Greer gets the message: Drugs and combat don't mix.. 31

Admissions Interview 3

At first Mr. Mendenhall's impersonation of a tortoise was regarded by staff as a healthy expression of levity. But that was three years ago. 7

A word of caution: Patients tend to take things quite literally on Unit 17. 33

"Baywatch" night 34

Believing himself to be a G.I. Joe action figure, Murray Hirschfield plots to escape Unit 17 by hiding under a plate cover... 41

Bill the janitor will soon require hip replacement surgery. Here's why....... 32

Burl Diggs practices for his first AA meeting........................ 8

By sheer coincidence the men in 19-C all enter REM-sleep at the same time. 44

Chamber music for the mentally derailed. 21

Charles Hobbes like giving wedgies, and the Plutchik brothers like getting them. ... 8

Check-In Time....................... 3

Coffee break is over. Please report to Stress-Management Workshop.............. 53

Colleagues would later conclude that Dr. Ramaswami had carried his systematic desensitization protocol a little too far. .. 37

Common use of shower stalls 55

Confidence building 16

Delusional George Toomer is starting to see his name everywhere. 49

Discharge Day (from the patient's view).. 57

Earlier in the day, Calvin Pomeroy found a quarter in his shoe, ate custard for dessert, and now... he dreams of heaven....... 53

Edgar Ebel's recurring eraser head nightmare 48

Egg jokes are popular at breakfast on Unit 17........................ 36

Ever since his appendectomy, Ira Nabbit confers with vital organs. 30

Every Friday evening, Lou Duffy's sister Lolly, a professional dancer, comes over from Club Kitty and licks her own breasts. .. 11

Every once in a while, Doug Tuttle envisions his confiscated household items. 13

Every Thursday evening, Myron Wainscott hosts a wall-locker party. But he doesn't participate... he watches............. 38

Every Thursday morning, Pastor Mullins, a minister of God's word, comes over from the United Methodist Church and reads from scripture. 11

Exercise builds self-esteem............. 49

Fed up with spot urine checks, Room 24-03 forms a posse. 54

Fights on Unit 17 concern inconsequential matters and are usually broken up by Wayne "the Wedge" McFarland........ 43

For one cigarette, Alfred J. Camden, a former attorney, will sue the government on your behalf. 12

For the third 4th of July picnic in a row, Marvin Cruikshank boldly attempts to smoke a firecracker. 26

For three nights now, Sonny Rodriguez has been getting his "Porkchop Hill" dream mixed up with that of his family dog. ... 45

Grateful Dead fan Spencer Diglio finds grizzled beard hairs and spectacles in his ice-cream and becomes agitated.. 17

Had he choice in the matter, Hugh Hemmings would prefer his recurring "Tet Offensive" dream to this: "Attack of the Childhood Toys"............................. 12

He heard about it in the army, but now, Ward Costello can only imagine just what the dickens "secks" is................... 39

Herb Weir, confident in his ability to pass through walls, regrets that he can only do it nude. ... 29
Hiding Meds ... 50
Holy War by night ... 19
Humor on Unit 17 ... 25
Improper use of shower stalls. ... 55
In a private moment, Floyd Howe figures out the universe. ... 10
Inter-disciplinary Treatment (Patient's View) ... 5
Inter-disciplinary Treatment (Staff's View) ... 5
Legal currency on Unit 17. ... 22
Leopold Krinsky describes his near-death experience to Dr. Dunne. ... 17
Lester T. Brentwood and Earl "Ripcord" De Salvo never miss Tuesday night ballet practice. ... 52
Level 1 patients fresh air break ... 34
Life on Unit 17 can sometimes turn out swell. ... 8
Lining Up for Meds ... 4
Lysle Karpinski receives two cartons of cigarettes in the mail and is promptly elected king. ... 29
Med student Laura Greenbaum begins her psych rotation on Unit 17. ... 47
Mr. Denby finds routine procedures to be quite delightful. ... 52
Mr. Mecklindale finally completes the Milton-Bradley special two-piece jig-saw puzzle. .. almost. ... 4
Night nurse Candy Pilquist finds time to erect a fanciful theme park from Doug Tuttle's belongings. ... 13
Nobody messes with Sharon Butts, the night nurse. ... 21
No shortage of "C" word euphemisms on Unit 17. ... 47
Nurse Cavaliero rethinks Mr. Weymouth's long-term obsession with "the big one." 23
Obsessive-Compulsive Disorder Clinic ... 38
Occupational therapy room by day ... 19
Once again, everyone ignores Big Bob Blauhoffer as he trys to swap his packet of decaf for 9 billion dollars. ... 18
Once Marines, always Marines. ... 45
Oral hygiene ... 42
Patty Hewlett, the only female patient on Unit 17, is afforded her own room .... sort of. ... 24
Perfume ain't just a river in Viet Nam. ... 42
Pizza Party. ... 6
Poignant moment on Unit 17. ... 54
Practical Joking on Unit 17. ... 23
Presidential debates. ... 28
Process Group ... 35
Proper use of shower stalls ... 55
Prozac, schmozac... it's Devil Dogs that these men crave. ... 40
Robert Ford, a new patient, quickly learns that on Unit 17, it's all in a name. ... 20
Self-confessed bigot, Mike Boyle, learns racial tolerance through an appropriate vehicle. ... 56
Some enigmas cannot be unraveled, like why Baldwin Grand will only sleep under the rec room piano. ... 41
Some of the chronic patients are starting to view Leonard Blevins in a whole new way. ... 27
Staff Dating. ... 9
Staff of Unit 17 (Aerial View) ... 46
Staff of Unit 17 (Frontal View). ... 46
Stress Management Group ... 22
Suicide watch. ... 28
Surgeons remove a benign tumor and actually find a homunculus in Ed Kesselbaum's head. ... 24
Thanksgiving Day ... 43
That Delmore Koontz can dramatically recite the entire dictionary in his underwear seems to impress nobody. ... 44
The brave men and horses of the First Cavalry salute their brethern. ... 7

The DVA-sponsored picnic affords Mr. McGunnigal a rare moment in which to liberate himself. 18

The Great Escape from Unit 17. 40

The most frequent sighting on Unit 17 is not Big Foot, Elvis or the Virgin Mary... It's Dwight Frye. 33

The reason nurse Donahue was fired 14

The Scuttlebutt Express. 39

The Unit 17 "Mentals" are 8 and 1 for the season, without ever shooting a basket. . . 36

The VFW-sponsored, donut and coffee party draws one attendee, Leonard Blevins, the new patient. 27

Tired of his green pajamas, Lionel Giacometti assembles an outfit to his own liking. . . 14

TV Room 15

Two new patients arrive. 32

Unit 17 swimming lessons 15

Unit 17 talent show finalists. 31

Vets from the 11th Marine Artillery Unit get to visit the hearing clinic. 26

Vital signs hi-jinx 37

Waiting for the American Legion-sponsored Pizza Party. 6

Waxy, baby, waxy 30

When those suffering from echolalia are paired, infinite regression inevitably follows. 16

While lining up for meds, Mr. Lewandofski has several out-of-body experiences at once. 51

With the spin of a record, half a dozen men remember what made them become warriors. 20

Work Incentive Program 9

www.ingramcontent.com/pod-product-compliance
Lightning Source LLC
Chambersburg PA
CBHW081501040426
42446CB00016B/3347